June Callwood

Terry Barber

ACTIVIST
SERIES

June Callwood is published by
Grass Roots Press, a division of Literacy Services of Canada Ltd.

PHONE 1–888–303–3213
WEBSITE www.grassrootsbooks.net

ACKNOWLEDGMENTS

We acknowledge the financial support of the Government of Canada through the Book Publishing Industry Development Program (BPIDP) for our publishing activities.

We acknowledge the support of
the Alberta Foundation for the Arts
for our publishing programs.

Editor: Dr. Pat Campbell
Consultant: Theresa Dobko
Image research: Dr. Pat Campbell
Book design: Lara Minja, Lime Design Inc.

Library and Archives Canada Cataloguing in Publication

Barber, Terry, date
    June Callwood / Terry Barber.

ISBN 978-1-894593-83-0

    1. Callwood, June. 2. Journalists—Canada—Biography. 3. Human rights workers—Canada—Biography. 4. Authors, Canadian (English)—20th century—Biography. 5. Readers for new literates. I. Title.

PE1126.N43B36456 2008   428.6'2   C2008-901986-5

Printed in Canada

Contents

The young people protest.

June Goes to Jail

It is 1968. Some young people live on the streets of Toronto. Others live in shelters. The police treat the young people badly. On July 10, people gather to **protest**. June Callwood joins them. The police try to break up the protest.

Some of the young people are **hippies**.

June watches the police arrest a young man.
July 10, 1968

June Goes to Jail

The police arrest a young man. June watches. She thinks the police are hurting the young man. She asks the police to stop. The police say, "This is none of your business." June will not leave.

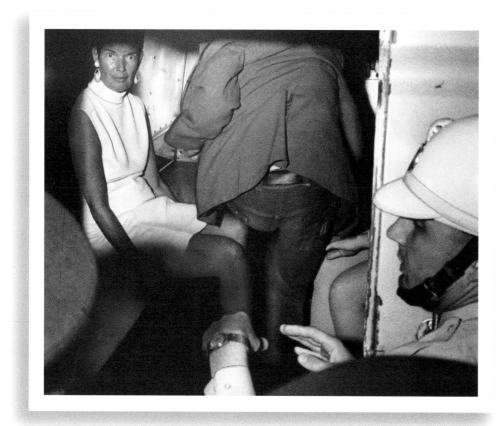

June Callwood sits in a paddy wagon.

June Goes to Jail

June is 44 years old. She is a well-known writer. People respect June. She thinks the police will listen to her. The police will not listen. They arrest June too. The police put June in a **paddy wagon**. They take her to jail.

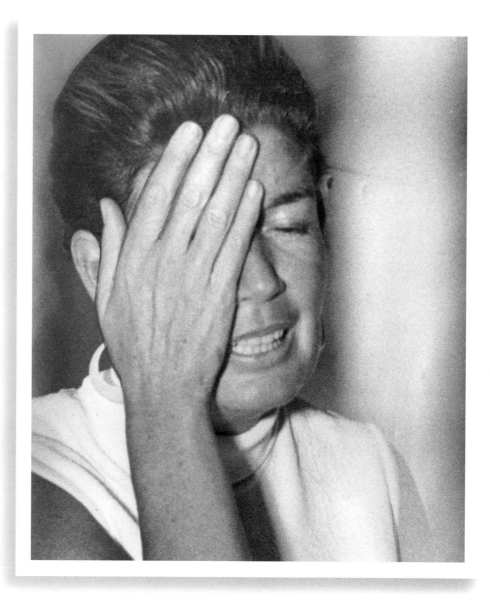

June is upset.

June Goes to Jail

The police put June in a very dirty jail cell. June cries. She thinks people will lose respect for her. June thinks no one will hire her again. June spends the night in jail. How did June get herself into this mess?

Don Jail is torn down in 1977. June helps to get it torn down.

June spends the night in Don Jail, Toronto

June Goes to Jail

June is in a mess because she cares. She cannot walk away from someone in trouble. She has to help. June also has a way of getting others to help. She will keep helping others for almost 40 years.

June becomes an activist after the protest and her arrest.

June's mother is Catholic. June's father is Anglican.

Byng Callwood,
June's father.

Gladys Lavoie Callwood,
June's mother.

Early Years

June is born in 1924. She grows up
in Belle River. Belle River is a French
Catholic town. June's family is
different. They speak two languages.
Her father speaks English. Her mother
speaks French. Her father and mother
have different religions.

June, age one.

Belle River, Ontario

Early Years

Belle River is a friendly community. People take care of one another. June learns that people need one another. June learns that people must help one another. She learns that the world is one big community.

June, age 12.

Early Years

June starts school. She is a good reader. She **skips** three grades. She is younger than the children in her class. Sometimes, she feels left out. But, June does not mind too much. June is a loner. She likes to play by herself.

June reads books when she feels lonely.

A girl gets ready to dive.

June's Deal

June joins a swim team. She likes
to compete. One day, June watches
a girl dive. The other girl makes a
poor dive. June cries out, "Oh, good!"
A boy hears June. He tells June she
is not kind.

June joins
the swim team
at age 11.

June's swim team, 1936.

June's Deal

June knows the boy is right. June feels shame. June makes a deal with herself. She will be kind to others for the rest of her life. She wants to be a good person. June is just eleven when she makes this promise.

These people do not have homes or jobs.
Queen's Park, Toronto, 1938

The Great Depression

The **Great Depression** takes place in the 1930s. June's life changes. Jobs are hard to find. Many people cannot pay their rent. Many people cannot buy food. The Depression makes life hard for June's family.

The Depression lasts from 1929 to 1939.

June stands with her mother and sister.

The Great Depression

It is 1937. June's father leaves his family. June lives with her mother and sister. They become poor. Sometimes they cannot pay their rent. They move from place to place. June learns how it feels to be poor and hungry.

June's mother is a **seamstress**.

June, age 16.

June's Calling

June's mother tells her to quit school. June needs to help support her family. June is only 16 years old. She gets a job at a newspaper. June works as a reporter. At first, the job is just a way to make money.

June quits school in 1941.

June writes 30 books.

June writes over 1,500 newspaper and magazine stories.

June's Calling

By the time she is 18, June loves her job. June finds her **calling**. She loves to write. June moves to Toronto in 1942. A large newspaper hires June. She makes $25 a week. The Depression is over. Life is good for June.

June, at about age 18.

June Callwood and Trent Frayne, 1943.

June Falls in Love

June meets another writer at work. His name is Trent Frayne. He is a sports writer. They fall in love. June marries Trent on May 13, 1944. They build a good life. They have two sons and two daughters.

June and Trent's children are Jesse, Jill, Brant, and Casey.

June Callwood at Digger House, 1968.

June, the Activist

June becomes an activist in the late
1960s. It is like a second job. June
supports many causes. She helps
homeless kids. She helps pregnant
teens. She helps people with AIDS.
June works hard to make life better
for poor people.

June helps
to start 50
groups.

June Callwood and her son Brant (centre) at Digger House.

June, the Activist

Many young people live on the street in downtown Toronto. They need a safe place to live. June wants to help the homeless teens. She helps to open a shelter for them. The _shelter_ opens in 1968. It is called Digger House.

June helps Jessie's Centre for more than 26 years.

June holds Yolanda at Jessie's Centre for Teenagers.

June, the Activist

Many teen moms raise children on their own. They need support. June joins a group of community leaders. They want young woman and their children to have good lives. They open Jessie's Centre for Teenagers in 1982.

Jessie's Centre is renamed the June Callwood Centre for Women and Families in 2008.

June sits beside Casey House.

June, the Activist

In the 1980s, some people die from a new disease. It is called AIDS. June helps to open a **hospice**. It is for people with AIDS. A person can die with dignity in a hospice. The hospice is called Casey House. It opens in 1988.

The hospice is named in memory of June's son. He is killed by a drunk driver in 1982.

June and Toronto's mayor look at the street sign.

A Woman to Remember

June lives her life to help others. She gets many honours. She gets the Order of Canada in 1986. A street is named after June. A park is named after June. June wins more than 50 awards for her work.

Some people say that June is Canada's **conscience**.

June Callwood, 1924-2007

A Woman to Remember

In 2003, June finds out she has cancer. She keeps working. June dies on April 14, 2007. More than 2,000 people light candles for June. They walk through Toronto's streets with June's family. June has made the world a better place.

Ontario's Premier and Toronto's mayor lead the candle light walk.

Glossary

calling: an inner urge to pursue an activity.

conscience: a feeling that one should do what is right.

Great Depression: a time of high unemployment, falling prices, and low wages.

hippy: a young person in the 1960s who rejects traditional society.

hospice: a home for sick and dying people.

paddy wagon: a van used by police to carry people they arrest.

protest: to complain about something.

seamstress: a woman who sews for a living.

skip: not attend.

Talking About the Book

What did you learn about June Callwood?

What words would you use to describe June?

What lessons did June learn when she lived in Belle River?

What challenges did June face in her life?

Some people say that June is Canada's conscience. What does this mean?

How did June make the world a better place?

Picture Credits